Contents

Aston Martin V12 Vanquish

British carmaker Aston Martin made its first sports car in 1914. Nearly 90 years later, the V12 Vanquish went on sale. Made from 2002 until 2006, it had a powerful engine and a body made of lightweight aluminium and carbon fibre. It was one of the fastest cars in the world.

DID YOU KNOW?

Superspy James Bond drove a V12 Vanquish in the movie *Die Another Day*. 007's car had rockets, guns and an ejector seat.

The V12 was built with Formula One-style gear-shift paddles behind the steering wheel.

Body panels were shaped by hand. The V12 Vanquish is popular with car collectors.

STATS & FACTS

LAUNCHED: 2002

ORIGIN: UK

ENGINE: 5,935 CC V12, FRONT-MOUNTED

MAXIMUM POWER: 460 BHP AT 6,500 RPM

MAXIMUM TORQUE: 400 LB PER FT AT 5,500 RPM

MAXIMUM SPEED: 306 KM/H (190 MPH)

ACCELERATION: 0-100 KM/H (0-60 MPH) IN 4.5 SECONDS

WEIGHT: 1.83 TONNES

COST: £158,000

Monster 47.5 cm wheels and high-performance tyres gripped the road.

BMW Z8

The Z8 combined power, speed and old-fashioned good looks. The car's design was based on the beautiful BMW 507 from the 1950s and its powerful V8 engine made it superfast. Without the electronic speed reducer, its top speed was 299 km/h (186 mph). The last Z8 was built in 2003.

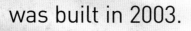

DID YOU KNOW?

At the time of launch, BMW promised to stockpile 50 years' worth of spare parts.

The Z8 safety system is called Dynamic Stability Control (DSC). If a driver takes a corner too quickly, the system's brakes slow down all four wheels.

Dials are in the centre of the dashboard and perform many functions. This keeps the interior uncluttered and gives the driver a clear view of the road.

Only 5,703 Z8s were built. About half of them were exported to the US.

STATS & FACTS

LAUNCHED: 1999

ORIGIN: GERMANY

ENGINE: 4,941 CC 32-VALVE V8, FRONT-MOUNTED

MAXIMUM POWER: 400 BHP AT 6,600 RPM

MAXIMUM TORQUE: 369 LB PER FT AT 3,800 RPM

MAXIMUM SPEED: 250 KM/H (155 MPH)

ACCELERATION: 0-100 KM/H (0-60 MPH) IN 4.8 SECONDS

WEIGHT: 1.58 TONNES

COST: £83,737 (ALL-ALUMINIUM CHASSIS AND BODY)

Bugatti Veyron 16.4

Volkwagen bought the legendary brand Bugatti in 1998 and launched the Veyron in 2003. A new model was produced in 2005. Inspired by the old Bugattis, it featured F1 safety technology so that the car could safely top 400 km/h (250 mph). It is so fast, it would lift off the ground if it weren't for the clever aerodynamics.

DID YOU KNOW?

A special edition Veyron 16.4 was created in collaboration with the fashion house Hermès. Unveiled at the 2008 Geneva Motor Show, it is so special it costs £1.5 million!

Ceramic brakes stop the car faster than it accelerates. It stops in 2.3 seconds from 100km/h (60 mph)!

The interior of the Bugatti Veyron 16.4 had to feel elegant, luxurious, and classic, while featuring the most modern technology.

To be fast, the Veyron 16.4 must be light. It is made from the lowest weight materials, including titanium, carbon and aluminium.

STATS & FACTS

LAUNCHED: 2005

ORIGIN: FRANCE

ENGINE: 8.0L W16-CYLINDER, QUAD TURBOCHARGER

MAXIMUM POWER: 1,001 BHP

MAXIMUM TORQUE: 1,922 LB PER FT AT 2,200–5,500 RPM

MAXIMUM SPEED: 407 KM/H (253 MPH)

ACCELERATION: 0-100 KM/H (0-60 MPH) IN 2.5 SECONDS

WEIGHT: 1,888 KG

COST: £1,087,000 (BASIC PRICE)

Chevrolet Corvette Z06

Chevrolet built the first Corvette in 1953, and it was soon the world's most popular sports car. The 2013 Corvette 427 Convertible is the fastest, most capable convertible in Corvette's history. It sold at a charity auction for £392,880.

This model belongs to the fifth generation of Corvettes (1997-2004). Chevrolet now makes sixth generation cars. The 2012 Z06 has an aluminium frame and carbon fibre components. It is hand-built and powered by a V8 engine.

DID YOU KNOW?
The Corvette is the official sports car of the Commonwealth of Kentucky.

The Corvette has a fighter-plane-style display. Speed, revolutions per minute (rpm) and fuel levels are shown on the windscreen.

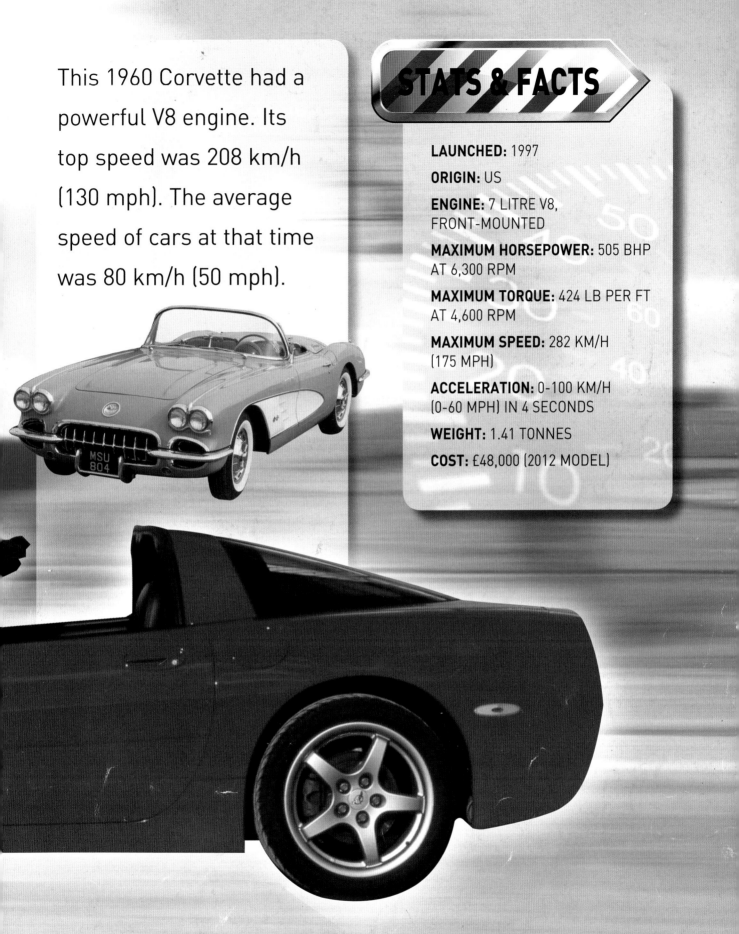

This 1960 Corvette had a powerful V8 engine. Its top speed was 208 km/h (130 mph). The average speed of cars at that time was 80 km/h (50 mph).

STATS & FACTS

LAUNCHED: 1997

ORIGIN: US

ENGINE: 7 LITRE V8, FRONT-MOUNTED

MAXIMUM HORSEPOWER: 505 BHP AT 6,300 RPM

MAXIMUM TORQUE: 424 LB PER FT AT 4,600 RPM

MAXIMUM SPEED: 282 KM/H (175 MPH)

ACCELERATION: 0-100 KM/H (0-60 MPH) IN 4 SECONDS

WEIGHT: 1.41 TONNES

COST: £48,000 (2012 MODEL)

Dodge Viper GTS

With twin stripes stretching across its body, the Viper GTS looked like it arrived straight from the racetrack. This is because it was designed by Carroll Shelby. He built the Shelby Cobras racing cars that broke records at the Daytona Speedway in Florida.

DID YOU KNOW?

The Viper GTS made the Guinness Book of World Records twice: for the fastest towing of a mobile home in 1998 and for the fastest run by a blind driver in 1999.

The enormous V10 engine was originally made for trucks. Lamborghini revised it to give it even more power – 450 brake horsepower (bhp).

Called the 'double bubble' because of its shape, the Viper was completely redesigned and replaced by the Viper SRT-10 in 2003. An all-new 2013 SRT Viper was unveiled at the New York Auto Show.

Early GTS models were a challenge to drive fast even on dry roads. Later models are easier to handle.

STATS & FACTS

LAUNCHED: 1996

ORIGIN: US

ENGINE: 7,990 CC V10, FRONT-MOUNTED

MAXIMUM POWER: 378 BHP AT 5,100 RPM

MAXIMUM TORQUE: 454 LB PER FT AT 3,600 RPM

MAXIMUM SPEED: 285 KM/H (177 MPH)

ACCELERATION: 0-100 KM/H (0-60 MPH) IN 4.5 SECONDS

WEIGHT: 1.29 TONNES

COST: £68,825

Ferrari F50

Ferrari makes some of the finest sports cars in the world. The F50 is one of the most exclusive models ever built. Just 349 cars were produced between 1995 and 1997 to celebrate the Italian legend's 50th anniversary. This incredible car boasted a slightly less powerful version of a 1989 Formula One engine.

DID YOU KNOW?

The F50 was very expensive. But you still had to roll the windows up and down by hand!

Underneath the car, the body is completely flat. The four exhausts stick out through holes cut into the rear, like a racing car.

The F50's body, doors and seats are made from lightweight carbon fibre.

The engine is in the middle of the F50. It powers the Ferrari to 100 km/h (60 mph) in under 4 seconds.

STATS & FACTS

LAUNCHED: 1995

ORIGIN: ITALY

ENGINE: 4,699 CC 60-VALVE V12, MID-MOUNTED

MAXIMUM POWER: 520 BHP AT 8,500 RPM

MAXIMUM TORQUE: 347 LB PER FT AT 6,500 RPM

MAXIMUM SPEED: 325 KM/H (202 MPH)

ACCELERATION: 0-60 MPH (0-100 KM/H) IN 3.7 SECONDS

WEIGHT: 1.23 TONNES

COST: AROUND £342,700

Jaguar XJ220S

In the late 1980s, British carmaker Jaguar built a supercar called the XJ220. The car was delivered in 1992 and its price was £415,000. Two years later, Jaguar produced a faster, lighter and cheaper version, the XJ220S.

The spoiler stretched across one of the widest sports cars ever made.

DID YOU KNOW?

In 1994, racing-car driver Martin Brundle reached 347 km/h (217 mph) in an XJ220S – at the time a record for a production car.

The XJ220S was built by TWR (Tom Walkinshaw Racing). The design was based on the XJ220C cars that took part in the Le Mans race in France in 1993.

STATS & FACTS

LAUNCHED: 1992

ORIGIN: UK

ENGINE: 3,498 CC TWIN-TURBO V6, MID-MOUNTED

MAXIMUM POWER: 680 BHP AT 7,200 RPM

MAXIMUM TORQUE: 527 LB PER FT AT 5,000 RPM

MAXIMUM SPEED: 350 KM/H (217 MPH)

ACCELERATION: 0-60 MPH (0-100 KM/H) IN 3.3 SECONDS

WEIGHT: 1.08 TONNES

COST: £293,750

The XJ220's aluminium body was replaced with carbon fibre to make the XJ220S even lighter.

Lamborghini Murciélago

Ferruccio Lamborghini was a wealthy Italian tractor maker. Unhappy with his Ferrari, he decided to build a better car. In 1966, Lamborghini made the first supercar, the Miura. In 2001, the company introduced the Murciélago. Production of the Murciélago ended in 2010. Its successor, the Aventador, was released in 2011.

DID YOU KNOW?

The Lamborghini logo is a charging bull. The Murciélago was named after a bull that fought so well in a bullring in Spain that its life was spared.

To reverse the Murciélago, most drivers flip open a door and sit on the edge of the car so they can look over their shoulders!

The roof and the doors of the Murciélago are made of steel. The rest of the car is made of carbon fibre.

STATS & FACTS

LAUNCHED: 2001

ORIGIN: ITALY

ENGINE: 6,192 CC V12, MID-MOUNTED

MAXIMUM POWER: 571 BHP AT 7,500 RPM

MAXIMUM TORQUE: 479 LB PER FT AT 5,400 RPM

MAXIMUM SPEED: 330 KM/H (205 MPH)

ACCELERATION: 0-60 MPH (0-100 KM/H) IN 4 SECONDS

WEIGHT: 1.65 TONNES

COST: FROM £163,000

The Murciélago has four-wheel drive and a safety system that slows the car down if it starts to lose its grip on the road.

McLaren F1

McLaren is known as the maker of Formula One cars. In 1993, the company decided to make the ultimate supercar. The result was the F1. It was the first production car to cost $1 million.

Only 106 cars were made between 1992 and 1998. Each machine took over three months to build.

The huge BMW engine fills the back. It powers the F1 to 160 km/h (100 mph) two seconds faster than a Ferrari.

DID YOU KNOW?

Without the electronic limiter, it reached 391 km/h (243 mph), a world record.

The central driving position is unusual for a sports car. So are the two rear seats.

STATS & FACTS

LAUNCHED: 1993

ORIGIN: UK

ENGINE: 6,064 CC 48-VALVE V12, MID-MOUNTED

MAXIMUM POWER: 627 BHP AT 7,400 RPM

MAXIMUM TORQUE: 479 LB PER FT AT 7,000 RPM

MAXIMUM SPEED: 386 KM/H (240 MPH)

ACCELERATION:
0-100 KM/H (60 MPH) IN 3.2 SECONDS
0-160 KM/H (100 MPH) IN 6.3 SECONDS

WEIGHT: 1.14 TONNES

COST: £634,700

Mercedes-Benz SL500

SL is short for 'Sport Lightweight' in German. Launched in 2001, the SL received a facelift in 2008. It has a new headlight system and a speed-sensitive steering system.

The roof folds into the boot at the click of a button. It takes just 17 seconds.

DID YOU KNOW?

An all-new SL class was launched in 2012.

The SL500 was inspired by the 190 SL, built in 1956. This classic was driven by Elvis Presley in the movie *GI Blues*.

A computer chip unlocks the car. Other features include satellite navigation and a TV monitor, both voice-activated!

STATS & FACTS

LAUNCHED: 2001

ORIGIN: GERMANY

ENGINE: 4,966 CC 24-VALVE V8, FRONT-MOUNTED

MAXIMUM POWER: 302 BHP AT 5,600 RPM

MAXIMUM TORQUE: 339 LB PER FT AT 2,700 RPM

MAXIMUM SPEED: 250 KM/H (155 MPH): LIMITED

ACCELERATION: 0-100 KM/H (0-60 MPH) IN 6.3 SECONDS

WEIGHT: 1.77 TONNES

COST: £68,000

Pagani Zonda C12 S

This car was designed by Horacio Pagani, who is from Argentina. It is named after a wind that blows from the Andes Mountains. The Pagani Zonda is perhaps the most exclusive supercar. Approximately 25 Zondas are built per year.

This C12 S model has a massive V12 engine.

If you drive a Zonda you have to travel light. The car doesn't have a boot!

DID YOU KNOW?

When you buy a Zonda, you get a pair of driving shoes made by the Pope's shoemaker.

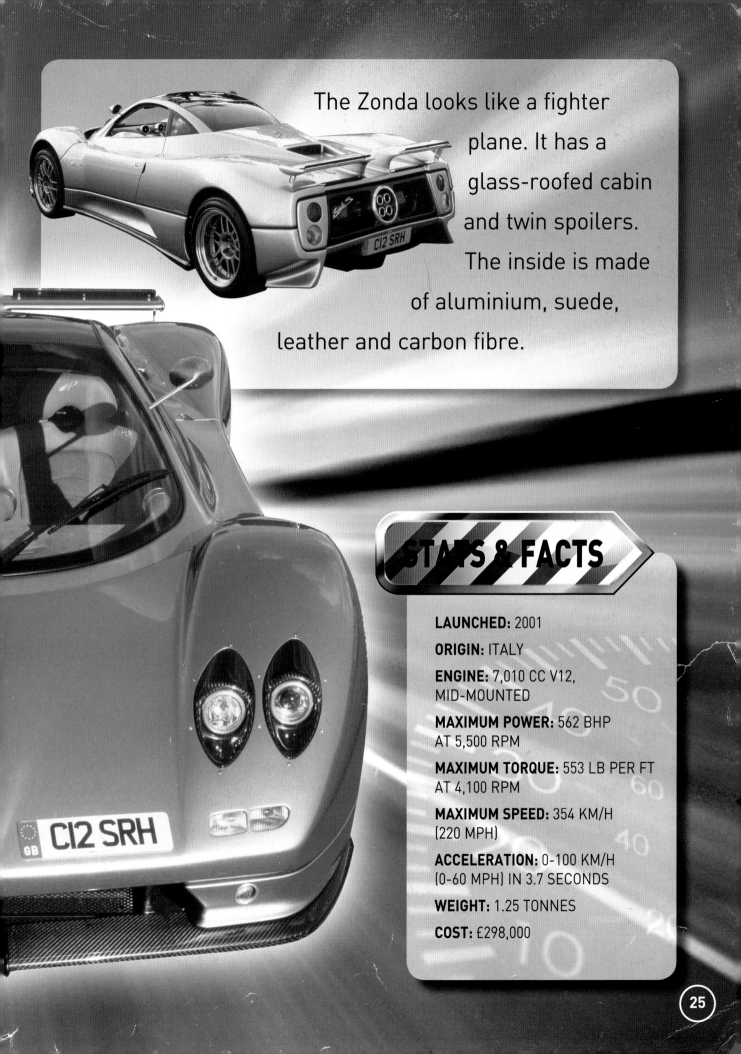

The Zonda looks like a fighter plane. It has a glass-roofed cabin and twin spoilers. The inside is made of aluminium, suede, leather and carbon fibre.

STATS & FACTS

LAUNCHED: 2001

ORIGIN: ITALY

ENGINE: 7,010 CC V12, MID-MOUNTED

MAXIMUM POWER: 562 BHP AT 5,500 RPM

MAXIMUM TORQUE: 553 LB PER FT AT 4,100 RPM

MAXIMUM SPEED: 354 KM/H (220 MPH)

ACCELERATION: 0-100 KM/H (0-60 MPH) IN 3.7 SECONDS

WEIGHT: 1.25 TONNES

COST: £298,000

Porsche 911 GT2

From the outside the GT2 looks like an ordinary Porsche 911 Turbo. But inside all of the luxuries have been removed to make it run like a racing car. The car has harder suspension, a roll cage, special brakes and lots of extra power!

DID YOU KNOW?

A GTS RS variant went on sale in 2010. It could top 330 km/h (205 mph). Only 500 cars were available in the US, and they sold out within hours.

The GT2 is 10 per cent more powerful and 7 per cent lighter than the 911 Turbo.

The spoiler and side panels have vents that cool the huge engine. There are also slats in the bonnet.

The GT2 accelerates to 298 km/h (186 mph) and brakes to a stop in less than 60 seconds.

STATS & FACTS

LAUNCHED: 2001

ORIGIN: GERMANY

ENGINE: 3,600 CC 24-VALVE TURBO FLAT 6, REAR-MOUNTED

MAXIMUM POWER: 455 BHP AT 5,700 RPM

MAXIMUM TORQUE: 459 LB PER FT AT 3,500 RPM

MAXIMUM SPEED: 317 KM/H (197 MPH)

ACCELERATION: 0-100 KM/H (0-62 MPH) IN 4.1 SECONDS

WEIGHT: 1.44 TONNES

COST: £110,000

TVR Tuscan

The TRV Tuscan is a sports car that was manufactured in the United Kingdom from 2000 to 2006. The car was made as light as possible and had a huge engine. As a result, it was amazingly fast and cost less than its rivals.

DID YOU KNOW?

John Travolta drove a purple Tuscan in the 2001 movie *Swordfish*.

To get into the Tuscan, drivers pressed a button under the sideview mirror. To get out, they twisted a knob in the car.

The roof and rear window could be removed and stored in the boot. There was even space left over for suitcases!

The engine filled most of the space under the bonnet.

STATS & FACTS

LAUNCHED: 2000

ORIGIN: UK

ENGINE: 3,605 CC 24 VALVE INLINE 6, FRONT-MOUNTED

MAXIMUM POWER: 350 BHP AT 7,200 RPM

MAXIMUM TORQUE: 290 LB PER FT AT 5,500 RPM

MAXIMUM SPEED: 290 KM/H (180 MPH)

ACCELERATION: 0-100 KM/H (0-60 MPH) IN 4.4 SECONDS

WEIGHT: 1.1 TONNES

COST: £40,000

Glossary

ACCELERATION The act of making a car go faster using the accelerator pedal.

BHP Brake horse power: the measure of an engine's power output.

BODY Outer part of a car that covers the chassis and engine.

BRAKES Part of a car used to slow it down.

CARBON FIBRE A modern lightweight material used to make cars.

CC Cubic capacity, the measurement used for the size of an engine.

CHASSIS The part that holds the engine, wheels and body together.

CONVERTIBLE A car having a top that can be lowered or removed.

CYLINDER The part of the engine where fuel is burned to make energy.

DASHBOARD The panel behind the steering wheel that usually contains the speedometer and other dials.

DYNAMIC STABILITY CONTROL A driver aid that can safely brake any or all four wheels.

ENGINE The part of the car where fuel is burned to create energy.

EXHAUST Pipe at the back of the car that lets out poisonous gases made when petrol is burned. The exhaust is also used to reduce engine noise.

FORMULA ONE Famous car racing championship.

FOUR-WHEEL DRIVE A car that has power delivered to all four wheels.

GEARS System used to allow a car to go faster or slower safely without damaging the engine.

GEAR-SHIFT PADDLES Levers on a steering wheel used to shift gears up and down.

NOSE The front end of a car.

RADIATOR A device through which water or other fluids flows to keep the engine cool.

ROLL CAGE A metal framework within a car to prevent it from being crushed if it turns over in an accident.

RPM Revolutions (revs) of the engine per minute.

SATELLITE NAVIGATION A system that tells you where your car is and lets you plot a route to any destination.

SPOILER A lightweight panel attached to a car to prevent the vehicle from lifting up at high speeds.

SUPERCAR A high-performance, high-cost production car.

SUSPENSION Springs and shock absorbers attached to a car's wheels, giving a smooth ride even on bumpy surfaces.

TAIL The rear of the car.

TORQUE The force with which engine power can be delivered to a car's wheels.

TRACTION CONTROL A driver aid that helps tyres grip the road.

TYRE A rubber wheel covering filled with compressed air.

V8/V12 The engine size given in number of cylinders.

V/INLINE/FLAT The arrangement of the cylinders in the engine.

VALVE Device that controls the flow of petrol into the engine.

Index